MODERN
HomeMaker

Creative Ideas for
Stylish Living

SARAH ROSE INCH

Contents

Introduction
  Make Life Beautiful. 7

Meet the HomeMaker 9

Sarah's Design Essentials 10

Designing a Life Together 13

1

MAKE Yourself at Home:
*Deconstructing Design,
Room by Room*

Room by Room. 15

The Bathroom. 17

The Bedroom 23

The Dining Room 29

 Children's Room 35

The Kitchen 41

The Living Room. 47

The Mudroom. 53

The Potting Shed 59

The Utility Room 65

2

MAKE a Memory:
Celebrating in Style at Home

Celebrating in Style at Home 71

Backyard Dream Wedding 73

Flower-Arranging Party 81

Holiday Brunch. 89

Children's Birthday Party 97

3

MAKE It Beautiful:
Styling School with Sarah

Styling School with Sarah 105

Arrange a Fresh Floral Centerpiece . . . 106

Bring the Indoors Out 110

Cozy Up with Candles 114

Create an Inspiring Workspace 118

Make a Bed (the Right Way) 122

Plant a Terrarium 126

Plant a Window Box 130

Set the Mood with a
   Creative Tablescape 134

Style a Bar Cart 138

Style a Coffee Table 142

Style a Cozy Guest Room 146

Style a Mantel 150

Style a Bookcase 154

Warm Up a White Room 158

Make a Market Bouquet 162

Wrap a Gift 166

4

MAKE a Plan:
Creative Tools for Organizing

Creative Tools for Organizing 171

Keeping Things Tidy 173

Declutter Checklist 175

Pantry Checklist 177

Glassware 179

Table Setting 181

Party Checklist 183

Furniture Styles 185

Notes 187

Index 188

INTRODUCTION

Make Life Beautiful

A house is simply a structure built to live in, but a home provides comfort, refuge, and love. That feeling doesn't happen on its own; it is made.

While the term "homemaker" has been around for many decades to define someone who manages the domestic details of life, we'll look at it a little differently in this book. A modern homemaker is anyone who has a passion for design and believes that the home environment can have a profound impact on well-being. A modern homemaker can be married or single, a homebody, a traveler, an entrepreneur, a mom, or anyone in between.

The most-welcoming spaces reflect the host's personality and make guests want to kick off their shoes and stay for a while. These homes not only look good but are also comfortable. They feel relaxed because the homeowner has put great care into the details. At our house, we encounter a lot of last-minute entertaining. To make life less stressful when those impromptu visits happen, I keep a variety of beverages and fresh fruit, nuts, and cheese on hand. I pull some pretty glasses out of the cabinet, arrange the snacks on a beautiful wooden board, and, voilà, instant appetizers! When I want to take it further, I'll snip some flowers from the backyard, light candles, and put on relaxing music. These simple tasks help me feel at ease while entertaining.

Beyond functionality, it's important to consider how your home makes you feel. A pile of pretty books on the coffee table, a vintage crock holding fresh flowers, the smell of a wood-burning fire, vintage art you've collected over the years—these items create a feeling of joy in your home. Take this same concept and apply it to the people who live with you. How will the spaces you create for your kids make them feel? Do you have an area for them to learn and be creative? Is the furniture in your home visually appealing while also allowing your family to feel comfortable? Thinking about these feelings and incorporating them into your design is what being a modern homemaker is all about.

You do not need a formal art degree to design your home. The eye can be trained. I hope that these pages inspire you to try something new, spark your passions, and guide you in confidence to make a home that you and your family and friends will love and enjoy.

Happy HomeMaking,

Sarah

Meet the HomeMaker

SARAH ROSE INCH

Where are you from?

I'm from a small town in Adams County, Pennsylvania called New Oxford, also known as the antique capital of Pennsylvania. I now live in York, Pennsylvania, where my husband grew up and our businesses are rooted, but my parents and family members are still just a short drive away to that small town.

Tell us about your family.

My husband, Jeff, and I have three children; Jozlyn, River, and Dawson. We also have an English cream retriever, a teacup Pomeranian, two goats, four sheep, a highland cow named Perry, and occasionally a gecko or two! I'm never quite sure what new four-legged family member will arrive at the house at any given time.

How did you get into interior design?

Growing up a cabinetmaker's daughter, I developed an eye for design and a passion for the home industry. I watched my dad design and build beautiful kitchens and living spaces for clients, and even learned how to use the tools in his shop. I was also inspired by Mom, who always had a knack for decorating.

How would you describe your design style?

I don't believe in having one specific design style. Instead, I design based on the era and architecture of a home and its surroundings. I also love to combine current trends and modern furnishings with vintage pieces. It's a blend that feels fresh yet timeless.

What does being a Modern HomeMaker mean to you?

The emphasis is on "maker." It's believing that the home environment affects our well-being and using creativity to create (or make) a space where the people who live there feel welcomed, comfortable, and inspired.

What is one item that you recommend splurging on for the home?

I always splurge on a good bed!

One item to save on?

Having young children means that the sofa will never look good for long. So, I always try to save on it.

Where do you find creative inspiration?

Getting out of my comfort zone always helps. When my husband and I travel, we make a point to visit beautiful towns with interesting architecture so we can learn and be inspired. I also love being on jobsites with our construction company. Over the years, we have renovated historic mansions, military bases, greenhouses, train stations, 200-year-old barns, warehouses, restaurants, old retail shops, antique malls, and more. Inspiration is everywhere, and I'm always looking.

You're an interior designer, shop owner, busy mama. How do you juggle it all?

It takes a village! I am blessed with a supportive family at home and a dedicated team at work. I owe a lot of credit to my husband, Jeff, who keeps me calm. Without him, all of this would still be a dream.

What is one design element you can't live without?

Fresh florals and foliage! They add warmth and charm while representing a season. They are timeless elements that complete a space.

SARAH'S
Design Essentials

With just a few staple items, you can make your house
warm, cozy, and welcome all through the year. Here are my essentials.
Try them out or mix in some of your own favorites.

A. Something Living: Plants

My go-to piece for filling an awkward
space in any room is a floor plant.
Bonus—they purify the air! The natural
color warms up a space without being
too bold. Be sure you have adequate
lighting and the appropriate size of
containers for your plants.

B. Something Vintage: Ceramics

Old wine jars, water pots, crocks,
and bowls are perfect vessels for
fresh flowers.

C. Something Textured: Pillows

Pillows pull a room together. Keep
the color palette consistent but blend
materials, sizes, and patterns. My
favorite textile types are mud cloth,
linen, and vintage embroidered.

D. Something with Color: Fresh Flowers

If permanent color in a room isn't your thing, fresh flowers should be. Incorporating the ever-changing colors of each season straight from nature is pleasing to the eye. Set a large vase of fresh flowers or branches on your coffee table and use the clipping to fill small bud vases for the bathroom.

E. Something Wooden: Furniture

Sitting a wooden bench against a white wall instantly creates a focal point. A gray sofa with white armchairs will make a living room feel dull until you add a reclaimed wood coffee table. The color tones of wood are endless. Don't be afraid to mix them in a room!

F. Something Shiny: Mirrors

Depending on its size, a mirror can have a dramatic effect on the feel of a room. I love adding floor mirrors at the end of a hallway and large brass mirrors above sofas and consoles to create a timeless look. When in doubt, add a mirror!

G. Something Modern: Art

Don't get me wrong; I am a huge collector of vintage oil paintings and framed landscape art, but there's always a place for modern art in a home. I love the ways it blends with antique furniture and ornate details.

H. Something Unexpected: Wallpaper

One of the easiest ways to liven up a space with color, texture, and pattern is adding wallpaper. I love to use it in kids' rooms for an unexpected pop of design. I like to keep the base pieces neutral and tie everything together with coordinating pillows and other accents.

DESIGNING A
Life Together

Home is a reflection of the heart.

When Jeff and I met, he lived in a house that he quickly renovated on a budget about a year before. It was pretty plain, and the goal was to have a temporary place until he found a farm to buy. Consequently, there wasn't much in it besides an old leather sofa, a television, and a few pictures (hanging too high on the walls).

A few months after we began dating, Jeff went on a trip, and I decided to surprise him by redecorating the inside of his house. I cleared out the kitchen clutter, put fruit in the bowls, added stools to the kitchen island, and put a coffee table in the living room. I also placed hand towels in the bathrooms, hung art to fit the walls, and added some scented candles.

To this day, he still remembers the way the house smelled when he returned and how the cozy environment made him feel. We later married, and that same house became our first home together. Over the years, we painted and repainted the walls, built furniture together, and eventually found our style of living.

We have designed and built commercial spaces and custom homes for many clients. Our taste and aesthetic evolve with each project, but our signature style always shines through. Jeff terms his design style as rustic modern. I like to mix styles, blending light colors and clean lines with modern and vintage accents.

I have to admit that Jeff is the more creative of the two of us. He's not afraid to step out of the box and run with a crazy idea. I'm the over-thinker. I have to be sure that all aspects of a design flow together. When Jeff has an over-the-top notion, I can usually integrate it with the rest of the project. So, the result is typically a cohesive space that is unique.

His "go big or go home" mantra applies to many areas of design. For example, I recently mentioned that I wanted a tall plant to put in the corner of our living room. Shortly after that, he came home with a flatbed trailer carrying the tallest and most full olive tree I've ever seen. I was in shock. He was persistent that it would fit (and it did), but I felt like I was living in a forest! So, the tree did not stay inside, but we made it work. It's now a beautiful focal point in our landscape.

Between the two of us and our various businesses, there is hardly a day that we aren't busy. With so much going on, it's essential that living be as convenient as possible. So, we designed our home to be a welcoming retreat that is spacious and functional for our family of five and great for entertaining. The key to keeping it all together is our support for one another. We keep it fun, share responsibilities, and help each other grow both at work and as a family.

Life and home aren't always perfect, but we try to remember the old adage, "Home wasn't built in a day." From our home to yours, happy homemaking!

Make Yourself at Home:

Deconstructing Design, Room by Room

This chapter will give you tips and ideas for designing nine rooms in the home, from the kitchen and bathroom to the bedroom and beyond. You'll learn how to borrow inspiration from a variety of design styles to create a home environment that is beautiful and welcoming.

It's time to make your house a home.

The Bathroom

Whether designing a small powder room or a luxurious home spa, there are a few things to keep in mind when planning a bathroom. To begin, consider who will be using the room. If it's a busy family bath, you might want to consider a double vanity. If it's a guest bath, be sure to include storage space for extra linens and toiletries. This section will show you how to outfit a modest-sized bathroom that doesn't skimp on style or necessities.

Update an older bathroom with sleek new light fixtures like these metallic sconces. It's the easiest and most cost-efficient way to modernize.

Scented candles and soothing bath salts can make any bathroom feel like a home spa. So keep them on hand and treat yourself to a relaxing soak in the tub.

The faucet may be practical, but that doesn't mean it can't be glamorous. This beautiful brass model adds sophistication and style to the room.

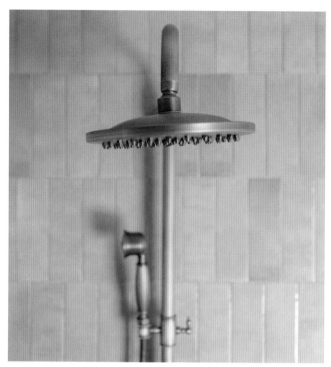

Hardware is a big part of any design story, so be sure to consider it up front. Here I selected beautiful brass knobs to coordinate with the other fixtures in the bathroom. I love how their sleek finish and modern design complement the warm wood cabinetry.

A combination rain shower with a handheld faucet like the one shown here may be a splurge but is worth every cent! The oversized head allows more water to flow, creating a luxury shower experience. And, the handheld faucet is excellent for bathing babies and pets!

There are so many options when it comes to selecting a bathroom mirror. If you are using sconces, position them so they are slightly higher than the center of the mirror.

Luxury for Less

You don't need an outrageous budget to create a beautiful bathroom. Simple design choices can make a significant impact. For example, create a focal point by swapping out the builders' grade frameless mirror for one that is elegantly shaped. Go for sleek brass fixtures and faucets. And upgrade your drawer knobs and pulls. You'll be amazed how small changes can make a big impact!

1. **Go for glass:** If your budget allows, a frameless (or semi-frameless) glass shower enclosure is a beautiful option. They do not require metal supports because they are made from thick, tempered glass. Therefore, they look clean and contemporary.

2. **Check your code:** Be sure to plan the appropriate number of electrical outlets on the basis of your expected usage and code requirements. When in doubt, consult with an electrician or check national and local regulations.

3. **Always accessorize:** Other than the kitchen, the bathroom is one of the most used rooms in the home. So, don't forget to go the extra mile when decorating it. Here, I hung a striking contemporary painting above the toilet and introduced black counter accessories to match it.

4. **Smart storage:** Keep your bathroom clean and clutter-free. Stowe personal grooming items in the vanity drawers, and add a small toilet tank basket to corral candles, matches, and other small items.

5. **Keep it fresh:** Good ventilation is a must for any bathroom. A high-quality fan or open window will keep the air circulating and reduce moisture created by hot showers.

The Bedroom

Most of us will spend one-third of our lives in the bedroom.
It's the first thing we see when we wake up and the last thing we see
before we go to bed. It is our sanctuary from the busy world,
yet one of the most overlooked rooms in the home. This section
will show you how to create a clean and serene haven filled with
natural textures to bring on a great night's sleep.

Don't throw your decorative
pillows on the floor at night!
Stow them in beautiful woven
baskets to keep them clean
and organized.

Layer on the coziness with
textured throw blankets.
They look great at the foot of
the bed and provide comfort
on chilly nights.

A bed is not made without a
throw pillow (or three)! Mix and
match different shapes, patterns,
and sizes to add personality and
style to your space.

Don't underestimate the impact of proper pillow pairing! Here we have combined square and lumbar pillows with stripes in varying sizes. The soft textures and neutral color scheme tie the design together.

Accent chairs are not just for the living room. This simple yet streamlined piece works perfectly to fill in the room's otherwise empty corner while also providing additional seating.

The bedside table is an essential element in any bedroom. Look for one with deep drawers large enough to store electronics and other personal items so they do not clutter your space.

This stylish black ladder is a creative solution for storing an extra throw blanket while also providing a punch of contrast, style, and industrial sophistication to balance the room.

Sweet Dreams

For this bedroom, the goal was to create a clean and serene space that promoted top-quality rest. We accomplished this by scaling the furnishings way back and incorporating a few statement pieces that are both functional and beautiful. The result is a clutter-free space that allows the homeowners to exhale when they climb into bed at the end of their busy day.

1. **Canopy dreams:** A canopy is the ultimate luxury piece for any bedroom. This modern design adds structure, height, and elegance to the space, while the slender construction and creamy-white finish keep it from taking over.

2. **Make a statement:** Editing is everything, my friends. Don't overpower your bedroom with lots of furniture. Commit to a few statement pieces and go bold with them, as we did with this handsome dresser.

3. **Go green:** Nothing adds life to a space like plants, flowers, and seasonal greenery. I love to incorporate large pots in the bedroom where they look great and can help filter toxins out of the air.

4. **Invest where it matters:** A good night's sleep is priceless, and the bed linens you select can make a world of difference. Invest in the best quality you can afford, and look for natural fibers that are breathable, comfortable, and durable.

5. **Find your footing:** A patterned rug is an excellent starting point for developing a color scheme. Here I started with the rich plum, brown, and ivory tones in the carpet and pulled them through the other elements in the room.

The Dining Room

A good meal is about so much more than food.
Dining-room design is about creating an experience where
those around your table feel welcome. Here are some tips to
help you create an inviting space that promotes connection, comfort,
and conversation, no matter the size of your home.

If you have one set of dishware, let it be white. White (or light) dishes let the food take center stage and pair well with any décor style. There's a reason most restaurants use them!

Your table is not complete without a centerpiece. Have fun arranging fresh flowers or invest in high-quality faux stems that look great all season long.

For easy, elegant, and affordable table décor, fill a decorative bowl with fresh fruit. I love to use pears since they symbolize sustenance and abundance—a perfect theme for holiday dining.

A handsome bar cart is the perfect modern accessory to have adjacent to your dining room. Use it to store overflow dishes, after-dinner drinks, or even dessert.

Mix high and low elements to create a collected look that is elevated without feeling formal. Here we paired classic white dishes and rattan-wrapped glasses with glamorous gold cutlery.

A beautifully arranged dinner table, set in advance, makes guests feel welcome. Consider the seating plan prior to your event if your guests are not yet acquainted.

No dedicated dining space? No problem. A cozy nook or even kitchen island functions perfectly for modern families. It's not about where you sit; it's about how you spend your time together.

(4)

An Open Concept

The way we use the dining room has changed over the years. Many busy families are opting for on-the-go dinners around the kitchen island vs. formal sit-down meals. Here are some design ideas for combining the best of both worlds with a sophisticated open-plan concept.

1. Let there be light: Natural light can change dramatically throughout a meal. Therefore, it's important to have good lighting. Select a statement fixture that is in proportion with the size of your table.

2. Table your discussion: The dining-room table is perhaps the most important piece of furniture in the home. When planning, remember to accommodate for moving chairs in, out, and around the room.

3. Go bold with beams: Removing walls to create an open concept often means living with an exposed beam. Here we painted the beam black to make it a major focal point. We used the same color on the chairs, light fixture, and adjacent door to establish unity in the design.

4. Be open-minded: The trend toward open concept does not mean that you have to sacrifice elegance. Use consistent paint colors and flooring materials to establish design continuity throughout the space.

5. Put the set aside: The secret to creating a collected look is to buy your chairs and table separately. Here I paired modern farmhouse chairs in black with a natural-wood table. The result is a room that looks like it evolved over time vs. coming straight off the showroom floor.

Children's Room

A child's room is so much more than a place for your little one to sleep. It's where they dream, learn, and play. So whether you are creating space for a newborn baby, busy toddler, or growing teen, it's important to design around the child's needs. Be sure to involve older children in the design process and have fun creating a magical space together.

You can never have too many baskets in a child's bedroom. Use them to organize toys, books, and laundry.

Hooks and hangers encourage little ones to keep their room tidy. Be sure to install them at kid-sized heights for easy cleanup.

Include your child in the design process. It allows them to express their personality and create a room they will love.

Give kids a soft place to land with fluffy pillows and soft bedding. Not only will they feel comfortable and secure, but you'll also be nice and cozy during story time!

A child's bedroom is not a showroom. So, include books and other items that spark their imagination, such as crayons and other art supplies.

Think long term when selecting furniture for your child's bedroom. You'll be surprised just how quickly they grow out of small dressers and toddler beds.

Children need to be inspired. My daughter loves flowers just as much as her mama, so we always have fresh blooms in her room. It's good to wake up to something beautiful!

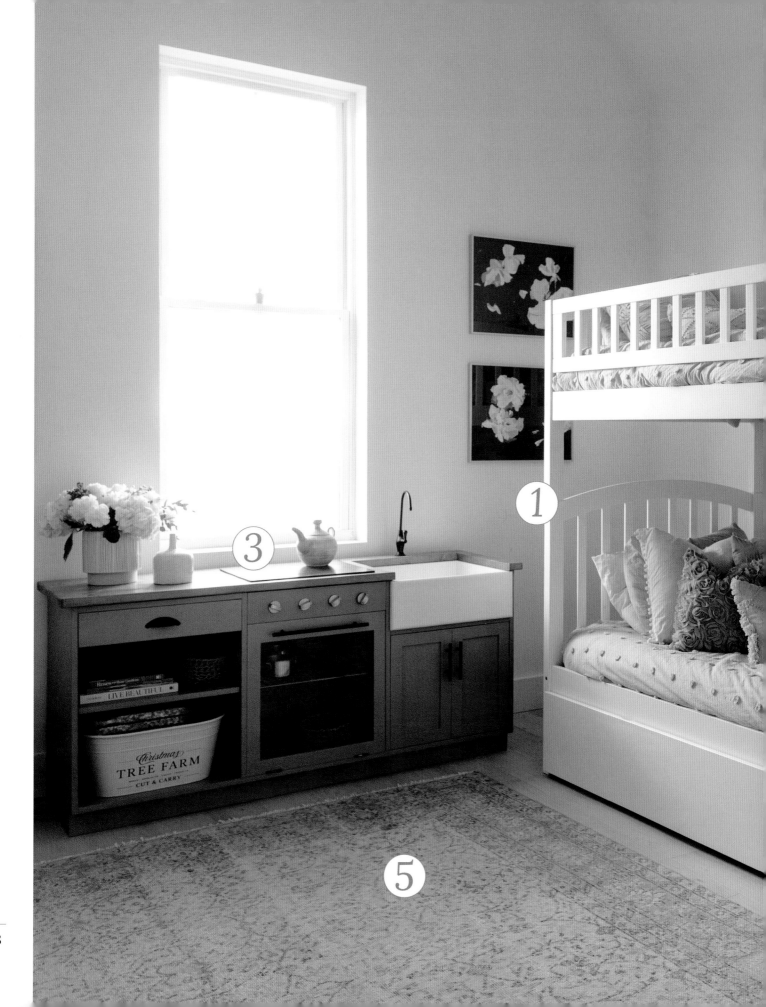

Let Them Be Little

Designing a child's room is one of the most joy-filled decorating projects, but it can also be a little daunting since their needs change so quickly. That's why I always recommend thinking long term. Keep the walls and significant furniture investments (like the bunk bed shown here) in a neutral color so that they can transition as the child grows and their interests change.

1. **Double the fun:** Bunk beds are great for sleepovers and a creative solution for families with multiple children. Be sure to install guardrails to prevent falls, and avoid proximity to ceiling fans, windows, and blinds.

2. **Step it up:** Bunk beds are available with staircases or ladders. Staircases such as the one shown here provide extra storage, but ladders take up less room. Pick the one that is right for your child and the space available.

3. **Let them be little:** Your child's room can be beautiful while still being playful. Be sure to plan plenty of room for toys.

4. **Stowe away:** Talk about a space saver. This bunk has a trundle bed that slides out quickly and is perfect for overnight guests. If storage space is more important than extra sleeping accommodations, remove the mattress and use the area to store clothes or blankets.

5. **Room to grow:** Floor space is play space, so be sure to include as much as possible when designing for children. Place large furniture along the perimeter of the room and leave the center open. Don't forget to add a rug to soften the tumbles that inevitably happen!

The
Kitchen

The hardworking kitchen. We demand so much from it! We need it to be practical, well organized, and functional to support our busy lives. But we also want it to be beautiful, comfortable, and welcoming as the central gathering spot in our homes. Thankfully, you don't have to sacrifice one need over the other. Let's look at how we accomplished this in a recent high-end renovation.

Keep frequently used items like hand soap and scrub brushes neatly corralled and within arm's reach of the sink.

If you do a lot of cooking, look for a high-arc faucet like the one shown here. It makes filling and cleaning large pots a breeze.

Accessories bring personality and style into your kitchen. This brass and marble pour-over coffee stand is both practical and beautiful!

Balance is what brings this gorgeous kitchen design to life. This apron front sink works beautifully to break up the long line of matte black cabinets and perfectly complements the modern metallic hardware.

This kitchen's marble countertops and glazed ceramic backsplash pair perfectly with the expansive six-burner gas range, complete with smart technology.

Small counter nooks and glass-front cabinets are perfect for showing off collections. Be sure to keep them tidy and change your items seasonally.

Move over stainless — matte black is now the trending finish for high-end kitchen appliances. I particularly love how this model does not have an exterior water dispenser. It keeps the overall look sleek, clean, and modern.

What do you call that style?

Don't get caught up in giving your design style a label. For example, this gorgeous high-end kitchen is a little rustic with the exposed wood ceiling and deep apron sink. But, it's also thoroughly modern with sleek black appliances, glamorous brass hardware, and glazed ceramic tile. When you understand how to balance elements, you can successfully draw from multiple design styles to establish a unique look.

1. Wood is good: We added a wood plank ceiling to keep this modern kitchen from feeling cold. The natural finish is warm and rustic and perfectly balances the hard surfaces. Notice how we repeated the wood accents on the beam above the oven and the island's base.

2. Build to last: Everyone's budget is different, but consider custom cabinetry if it's within reach. You can personalize your cabinets to fit your space and add long-lasting value to your home.

3. Mix it up: Don't be afraid to mix materials, especially when you want to create a one-of-a-kind design. We mixed high-end appliances and sleek brass hardware with Shaker cabinets and black farmhouse bar stools in this kitchen. The result is a showstopping kitchen that doesn't feel too fancy to cook in!

4. Let's talk about that pot filler: It creates a beautiful focal point above the oven and helps reduce congestion at the sink when preparing large meals.

5. The extended island: This extra-long island is the absolute crowning jewel of the kitchen, with room for five stools on one side. It's large enough to spread out an impressive holiday buffet, yet cozy enough for casual family dinners.

The Living Room

Living rooms are designed for gatherings and therefore tend to be one of the largest rooms in the home. For that reason, they can also be one of the most intimidating to decorate. In this section, I will show you how to create a comfortable living room that blends modern and contemporary elements to create a lived-in look that still feels refined. Balance is everything when it comes to sound design, and I'll show you how to achieve it!

Comfortable seating is a must in your living room. Invest in the best quality you can afford, and select neutral colors that won't go out of style.

Don't underestimate the power of decorative accents. Interesting items like this wooden knot can inspire conversation and bring warmth and character into a room.

Throw pillows aren't just for comfort. They add style and interest to your living room. Mix various patterns and textures to create a layered look that feels approachable.

These sculptural chairs blend cool contemporary style with casual comfort. The deep cushions and round shape invite people to sink in and relax, while the muted color is soothing to the eye. They are basically the furniture equivalent of a warm hug!

Mirrors are always a good idea. They come in a variety of shapes and sizes and blend seamlessly with other design elements. For example, this round mirror with its matte brass frame reflects natural light into the room and balances well with the seagrass bench below.

A built-in bookcase is a perfect place to showcase small collections in an otherwise minimalistic room. Here we arranged favorite books, small works of art, and beloved travel souvenirs to add a personal touch to the room.

Dark leather sofas are timeless and lend an air of rugged sophistication to any room. Here we have balanced the dark color out by placing the couch in front of a large window framed with light-colored drapery.

The Gathering Room

The most critical step in designing a living room is to determine how you will use it. Here I will share the design inspiration for our relaxed gathering room, which is comfortable enough for everyday living but roomy and stylish enough for entertaining. Remember, form always follows function!

1. **Mix and match:** The white walls and light furniture soften the bold black door that punctuates the room.

2. **Room to move:** At the center of this relatively open living room is a hardworking wooden coffee table that blends with the other natural elements in the room. We left plenty of space around it so that family members (especially toddlers) could move about freely.

3. **Wall power:** Art is what completes a room, so don't ignore your walls. This moody landscape ties in perfectly with the other dark accents in the room to create a sense of drama. The accepted rule of thumb is to position the art so that the center is 60" from the floor.

4. **Floor plan:** An area rug defines your seating space and adds a layer of comfort over wood, tile, or laminate floors. To make the most of your investment, look for timeless designs and plush textures made with durable materials.

5. **Accessorize:** Once the large furnishings are in place, it's time to get creative with lighting and accessories. We completed this room with a stylish gold tripod lamp.

The Mudroom

Many busy families have traded fancy entryways for hardworking mudrooms. They are one of the biggest trends in home design. Whether you have a dedicated room like the aspirational one shown here or a cozy corner borrowed from the entryway — a mudroom will keep your family organized and your home tidy. So let's take a look at some essential ideas to establish a functional and beautiful mudroom, no matter the size of your space.

Baskets and mudrooms are a match made in heaven. Use them to organize small items like mittens, phone chargers, and mail.

Don't bring wet shoes and boots into your main living space. Instead, park them in the mudroom where they can dry out.

Beautiful hats are an investment. Protect yours by hanging it on a hook in the mudroom, where it will always be ready to wear.

The mudroom is a versatile space that you can design to suit your needs. For example, if you love gardening, devote an area of your mudroom to organize small tools, garden baskets, and gloves, so they are ready for your next trip into the yard.

Shoes, boots, and sneakers can quickly take over a home—especially if you have a large family! To corral the chaos, devote a place in the mudroom to store footwear. You'll be amazed at how leaving shoes at the door cuts down on clutter (not to mention dirt).

Hooks are the humble but hardworking secret ingredient in the mudroom. They come in various sizes and styles to complement your mudroom design. And, they are perfect for organizing oversized items like hats, coats, and backpacks.

The mudroom is most likely the first room you will see upon entering your home, so take time to make it beautiful. Small additions, like houseplants and framed art, don't take up a lot of room and breathe life into the otherwise utilitarian space.

Grab and Go!

The mudroom is a transitional space that takes us from the outside world to the interior of our home. It's where we store bags, jackets, shoes, and even gardening tools. Here are some tips and ideas for establishing a functional and beautiful mudroom that will help you shed the day before entering your main living space.

1. Function first: When designing a mudroom, it's essential to start with practical matters. Use durable materials that conceal dirt and hold up to high traffic, like the brick flooring shown here.

2. Closed storage: If space and budget allow, it's wonderful to have a combination of open and closed storage in your mudroom. Here we have installed closed-door closets, upper cabinets, and drawers. The result is a streamlined look that feels clean and calm.

3. Locker room: A mudroom with designated cubbies is a game-changer for busy families. Having a dedicated space to store everyday items helps kids get off to a good start in the morning. Just grab and go!

4. Seat yourself: Seating is essential in a mudroom, where shoe changing is standard. Here we have two options, a sturdy bench built right into the cabinetry and a freestanding one that adds a touch of French country flair to the space.

5. Personalize it: A hardworking room does not have to lack character, grace, and style. Bring plants, art, and personal accessories into your space. Here, we added greenery and a framed landscape to the upper shelves, and hats on the iron hooks. Everything the family needs is within reach, and the room looks terrific.

The Potting Shed

In the long winter months, many gardeners await the arrival of spring and look forward to spending time in their garden shed. Whether sowing seeds, nurturing plants, or arranging fresh-cut flowers, I'll show you some creative ideas to transform an ordinary outbuilding into the she-shed of your dreams.

Bring the outdoors in with beautiful flowers picked right from your garden. They'll brighten up your space and make it smell amazing.

Keep a few woven baskets in your shed. They are great for stowing garden gloves, seed packets, and small tools.

Watering cans with long necks are perfect for reaching under the leaves of small potted plants. Bigger ones with sprinklers are great for larger containers.

A wooden stool performs double duty in the shed. It's not only a comfortable place to sit, it also makes a great plant stand.

Make room for kiddos! Gardening is so good for children. It teaches them about patience, responsibility, and caring for the natural environment. Welcome them to your potting shed.

Add character with vintage pieces. Antique wooden crates are lovely for storing potted plants. They stand up well to dirt and typically get better with age.

A humble shed can be a charming focal point in your yard when you add window boxes and landscaping. If a significant landscape job is not in your budget, consider potting evergreens. They will look great year-round, especially at the holidays' when you can string them with lights.

A Potter's Paradise

A potting shed has the potential to be so much more than just a practical place to store garden tools. Add a shelf of inspirational gardening books, and it becomes a library. Fill a box with beautiful stationery, and it becomes a writer's studio. Decorate it with flowers, herbs, and plants, and it becomes your personal place to connect with nature.

1. **Let the sunshine in:** If you plan to spend a lot of time working in the shed, be sure to position it so that the windows are in the path of the sun.

2. **Setting the bar:** If your shed does not come with a workbench, you can build your own or commission a local carpenter to make one from inexpensive lumber. The ideal height is 36″, similar to a kitchen counter.

3. **Contain yourself:** There are so many choices when it comes to planting pots and containers. I recommend having a variety on hand so that you have options for different types of plants. I love vintage clay pots for their Old World charm.

4. **Against the wall:** Hooks and dowels are convenient in the gardener's shed. You can install them on walls to organize often-used gardening tools, so they are easily within reach. Don't forget to reserve a hook for your favorite garden hat!

5. **Hydration station:** Water is an essential element if you plan on doing a lot of gardening in your shed. If you do not have access to running water, be sure to keep a variety of watering cans on hand so you can hydrate flowers, plants, and seedlings.

The Utility Room

If you ask many busy homeowners what their favorite "bonus" room is, you might be surprised by the answer. It's not a media room or even a home gym; it's a utility room! Having a clean, organized, and well-outfitted space to tackle daily chores can make everyday life immensely more pleasant, especially if you take the time to make it stylish like the one shown here!

Work smarter, not harder. Well-designed tools make cleaning chores go faster and last longer.

Reduce visual clutter in the utility room by decanting liquids into beautiful bottles.

Baskets are your best friend for organizing in the utility room. Use them to store folded cleaning cloths and other small supplies.

A wall-mounted dryer rack is a lifesaver in the utility room. It saves valuable floor space and is a perfect solution for drying delicate garments and those made of silk or wool.

This handsome sliding barn door takes up less floor space than a swinging door. And, it is easy to slide open or shut when the homeowner's arms are full of laundry!

A cement sink is a beautiful and durable choice for the utility room! It can hold up to dirty tasks like washing pets, planting pots, and soaking stained laundry.

Beauty Meets Utility

Household tasks like cleaning and laundry are a part of everyday life. So, why not take the time to make them more enjoyable? A beautifully designed utility room can have a significant impact on your outlook. When supplies are stocked, cleaning tools are organized, and your environment is pleasing, you'll find that weekly chores are more pleasant (and you might even enjoy them!).

1. **Be bold:** Utility rooms are a wonderful place to experiment with wallpaper! Because they are typically smaller spaces closed off from visitors, you can take a creative risk with a bold design. If you are feeling apprehensive, try a removable wallpaper.

2. **Stylish storage:** Always plan for more storage in the utility room than you think you'll need. Matching baskets look good when displayed on open shelving and can hold many items, from cleaning supplies and small tools to orphaned socks coming out of the dryer!

3. **Shelf it:** It's convenient to have a shelf above your washer and dryer. You can use it to keep laundry detergent, dryer sheets, and other often-used items close at hand. Decant your cleaning supplies into beautiful containers to reduce visual clutter.

4. **Great reflections:** If your utility space is dimmer than you would like it to be, brighten it up with a mirror. It will reflect the light and make the area feel more cheerful. I particularly love how this mirror's rustic frame ties in with the shelf, made from old barn wood.

5. **Houseplant happy:** Bring life into your utility with houseplants. Even a small potted plant can make the space feel more welcoming.

Make a Memory:
Celebrating in Style at Home

Home is much more than where we eat, sleep, and park our car. It's the backdrop to our life story and the place where we make memories. In this chapter, you'll find four creative party ideas to make the next gathering in your home genuinely unforgettable. In the end, it's not the furniture or the accessories people remember; it's the way you made them feel. So let's make a memory!

Backyard Dream Wedding

And so, the adventure begins...

A home wedding is perhaps the highest expression of creative homemaking. If you get the chance to host one, it's a serious commitment but does not have to cost a fortune. In this section, I'll share some creative ways that my husband and I transformed my parents' beautifully wooded backyard to create the wedding of our dreams without breaking the bank.

A ceremony marker, like this trellis decorated with floral garlands, creates a focal point in the yard and establishes a sacred space where the couple can exchange vows.

A nearby field or park is the perfect place to take wedding portraits after the ceremony.

Table décor does not have to be elaborate to be beautiful. For example, simple flower arrangements are the perfect centerpiece for an outdoor wedding.

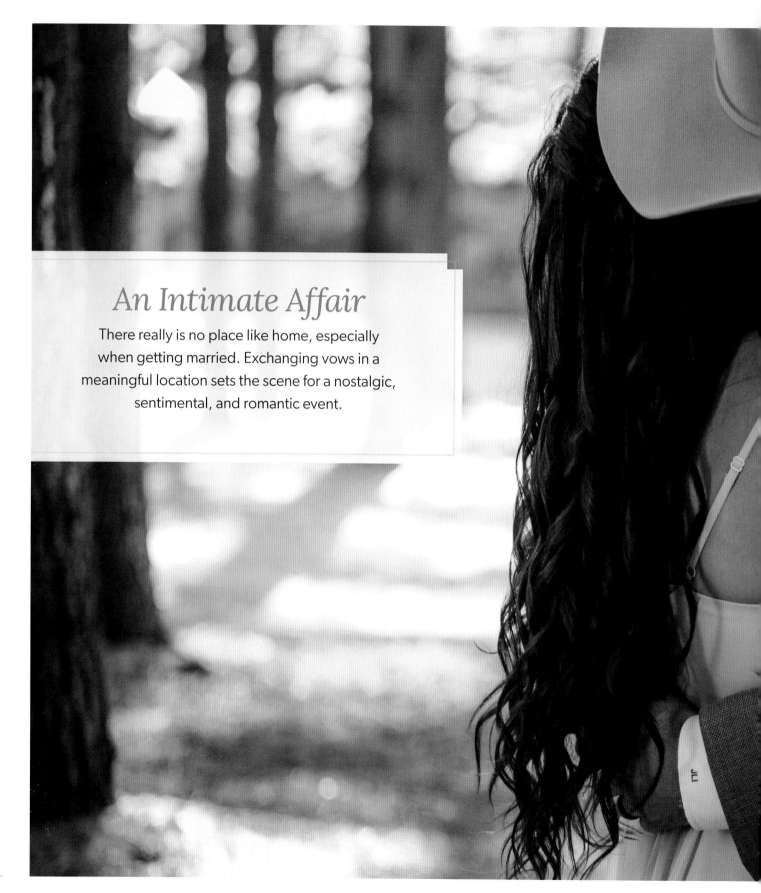

An Intimate Affair

There really is no place like home, especially when getting married. Exchanging vows in a meaningful location sets the scene for a nostalgic, sentimental, and romantic event.

(5)

Timber & Twinkle

You don't have to do much to improve upon Mother Nature. For our outdoor reception, we let the natural environment take center stage. We wrapped string lights around the tall trees and brought in long banquet tables to complement the rustic atmosphere. White linens and pale-peach florals elevate the look without getting too formal.

1. Food truck fun: Outdoor weddings are perfect for food trucks. They provide an experience for guests and make great photo backdrops. Plus, they can be more affordable than traditional catering, depending on the vendor.

2. String light canopy: There's just something special about string lights. They can make even the most humble space feel special. And, they are a perfect solution for lighting an outdoor wedding after the sun goes down.

3. Drama through repetition: A great way to make a major design impact while still keeping things simple is through repetition. Notice how the long row of floral vases creates a focal point without taking over.

4. Banquet of dreams: Long banquet-style tables create a stunning visual effect and are perfect for outdoor weddings. They evoke the casual feeling of a family dinner and encourage the guests to relax and enjoy.

5. Mixed seating: Antique mismatched chairs are a fun idea for an outdoor wedding! They create casual charm while providing a comfortable place for your guests to sit. Many rental companies can now supply them (or you can scour local flea markets).

Flower-Arranging Party

May your house always be too small to hold all of your friends.
—IRISH BLESSING

The only thing better than spending an afternoon with your girlfriends is doing it with buckets full of fresh flowers! This section will give you tips and advice for hosting a fun flower-arranging party. It's a creative entertaining idea that allows you and your besties the opportunity to spend time together, create memories, and make something beautiful.

The party is not complete without a signature cocktail (or mocktail). So, look for creative recipes like this blood orange and elderflower cocktail with a floral garnish.

Have a variety of vases and vessels available for your guests. You can buy them from a local shop or scour thrift and antique stores.

Encourage your guests to get creative. These are personal arrangements, not wedding bouquets! There's no right or wrong way to do it.

A Feast for Friends

Every moment matters, so don't wait for a special occasion to throw a party. Invite your girlfriends over for an afternoon of creative fun. Make a signature drink and unbox some delicious treats from your favorite local baker. Try cooking, crafting, or a home spa treatment if flower arranging is not your thing.

Make Your Own Flower Bar

Are you ready to host a flower-arranging party? Good! Start by setting up your flower bar. I like to provide eight to ten flowers and greens as fillers. Prep your flowers and place them in large pots filled with water (or lined wicker baskets as shown here). Provide vases and garden scissors for each guest and have plenty of water available.

1. Seeded eucalyptus: With sage-green leaves and clusters of seeds, this fragrant green is perfect for adding texture to a bouquet or flower arrangement.

2. Hydrangea: Always elegant and beautiful white hydrangeas are perfect for large arrangments. Pair them with other large blooms of similar scale.

3. Tulips: Tulips are a perennial favorite and come in a wide variety of colors. Arrange red ones to represent passion, yellow for friendship, and white for good health.

4. Roses: Your flower bar is not complete without at least one rose. The pale-lilac variety shown in the photo is one of the rarest colors and symbolizes enchantment.

5. Chrysanthemum: Long-lasting and affordable; it's no wonder chrysanthemums are a favorite flower for floral arrangements. They come in many shades and are especially popular in fall.

Holiday Brunch

All roads lead home for the holidays.

The holiday season is the perfect time to open your home to friends
and family. But if a formal dinner or late-night cocktail party sounds
a little overwhelming during the busiest time of the year—try brunch!
Brunch can be a surprisingly simple event to put together when you
plan ahead. Here I will share tips for a sweet and savory buffet complete
with all the holiday trimmings. Let's celebrate the season in style!

This festive holiday punch is aromatic, delicious, and easy to make. Simply combine two-thirds of your favorite dry red wine and one-third pomegranate juice in a glass pitcher. Add fresh slices of orange, a rosemary stalk, and top with sparkling water or club soda.

No buffet is complete without a bountiful fruit bowl (or two). Not only will this fresh bowl of oranges provide a healthy dose of vitamin C for your guests, but it will also look great on the buffet. Who doesn't love winter citrus?

Give your guests something to graze on, like these tasty bruschetta bites made with crusty ciabatta bread, basil leaves, ripe tomato, and fresh mozzarella. Bonus: they happen to match the red-and-green holiday décor.

Elevated Deliciousness

Individually packaged desserts allow you to spend more time mingling with your guests and less time serving them. These grab-and-go cheesecakes are a perfect example. Make them yourself by layering ingredients in a latched jar (available at most craft stores) or order them ahead from a local baker. Then, display them on an elevated tray with a hand-lettered sign and seasonal greenery for a finishing touch.

Light & Airy Holiday Style

Give your guests respite from the hectic holiday season with a leisurely winter brunch. Open your windows to let the natural light in, and scale your holiday décor back to fewer items intentionally arranged. Follow the below tips for more ideas.

1. **Change up your wall art for the holiday season.** The charcoal pine drawings provide a seasonal backdrop without demanding too much attention.

2. **Greens, always greens!** No buffet table is complete without seasonal foliage. Try swapping out traditional holiday florals with a vase of seeded eucalyptus. The minty scent will provide a subtle aroma that will not compete with your food.

3. **When in doubt, hire it out!** There is no rule that says you have to make the party food yourself. Connect with a local baker to order cupcakes, tiered desserts, and cookies ahead of time if it is within your means. Maybe they will even deliver!

4. **Don't forget to include essentials** like forks, spoons, small plates, and napkins on your buffet table. Get creative with your presentation, and don't be afraid to employ the high/low rule of decorating, like putting glamourous gold cutlery in a rustic wicker basket. The result is both casual and elegant at the same time.

Children's Birthday Party

The days are long, but the years are short.

Anyone who has children knows that time flies by too quickly. That's why it is so important to celebrate important milestones like birthdays. No matter how big or small, a themed birthday party is an opportunity to honor your child and strengthen family bonds. Here are tips and ideas for a super sweet clementine party that we organized for our daughter River's second birthday.

Create an adorable clementine garland by tying small orange balloons finished with green leaves to a length of kitchen twine.

Personalize your party with a cute sign. This sign is hand-lettered, but you can use stickers or make a custom design using an electronic craft cutter.

I'm blessed to have talented carpenters in the family who made this adorable market stand for River's party, but with some creativity, you could fashion something similar using a small cart.

Dessert Bar

Make your party extra sweet with a themed dessert bar. For our orange-themed event, I arranged citrus cupcakes, cake pops, and macarons on trays of various heights. Fresh oranges and seeded eucalyptus fill in empty spaces and add an elegant flair to the table.

A Super sweet Party

Dessert was the main course at our cutie clementine party! Here are the details about how I put together this themed buffet table.

1. **It's all about the cake:** The cake takes center stage on this buffet and is elevated with a simple wooden stand.

2. **Don't forget décor:** In addition to all of the delectable goodies, I added helium balloons to each end of the table. They are inexpensive and add a fun flair. Just be sure you have a car big enough to transport them (or do yourself a favor and get them delivered!)

3. **Level it up:** I love to use tiered trays on any buffet. Various serving levels allow you to offer more selection and choice to your guests.

4. **Keep it natural:** I love to use natural elements and a restrained palette to keep party décor from going overboard. Here, I used oranges and eucalyptus stems and even crafted a festive garland with wooden beads and fabric swatches.

Make it Beautiful:
Styling School with Sarah

Modern homemaking is about creative living. It's putting a personal touch into everything you do, with an effort to live life more authentically. This chapter will tackle projects great and small to provide information and inspiration to make your life even more beautiful.

ARRANGE A FRESH
Floral
Centerpiece

When it comes to fresh floral centerpieces, I am DIY all the way. Not only is it relaxing and fun to mix and match fresh flowers to create custom arrangements, but it's a total money saver. The best part is that you can create something that truly reflects your style versus a stuffy commercial piece that costs a fortune!

1. **Pick your vessel:** Think about where you will be setting your centerpiece, and pick a vessel that coordinates. Dining al fresco? A weighty rustic ceramic is a perfect match. Formal dinner party? Try cut crystal or vintage china.

2. **Gather your greens:** Whether you are purchasing from a farmstand or florist or harvesting from nature, be sure to collect a variety of blooms and foliage to create an interesting composition.

3. **Snip your stems:** Begin by prepping your florals. Snip each stem to your desired size on the basis of the height of your vessel, and remove any leaves on the lower half. Place your focal-point flower stems into the vase.

4. **Add the accents:** Variety is the spice of life. Pick a supporting flower that coordinates with your main bloom. Here we have paired a seasonal burnt orange mum to offset our pale pink rose.

5. **Have fun with filler:** With your focal florals set, it's time to fill your vase with smaller buds and greens. Look for berries and branches that complement, rather than compete with, your key ingredients.

Make a Design Moment: Styling School with Sarah

Al Fresco Dining

Nothing says casual elegance quite like a seasonal dinner in the great outdoors. Here, a weathered farm table, vintage wicker chairs, and soft linens are complemented by our fresh floral centerpiece and bowl of fruit. Invite your friends over and enjoy a long night of good food and great conversation.

BRING THE
Indoors Out

When designing your home, it's essential to think about how the interior and exterior relate to one another. A cohesive style between the two spaces is pleasing to the eye and establishes a sense of flow. Here I will show you how to design a beautiful outdoor space inspired by the indoors' color, texture, and warmth. It's time to bring the indoors out!

1. Cohesive colors: One of the easiest ways to create a cohesive design inside and out is through the use of color and texture. These burgundy hydrangeas arranged in woven baskets make the outdoor space feel welcoming and coordinate with the indoor color palette.

2. Paint it black: This bold black door makes a modern design statement and ties in with the beautiful black window frames. The color is repeated inside with black hardware and accessories.

3. Gorgeous garages: Garages, sheds, and outbuildings are used for a lot more than storage these days. So whether yours is for parking or bonus space, be sure to include it in your design process. We painted this gorgeous garage in black and added copper lighting to complement the cedar wood accents in the home.

4. Get comfortable: Even small porches or patios can vastly expand your living space when outfitted with comfortable furnishings. Here, a cozy teak settee covered in stylish outdoor fabric makes a beautiful and comfortable place to rest year-round.

Outdoor Living

You don't need a massive yard or deck to enjoy outdoor living. This cozy covered porch, complete with a small garden, is a perfect place to enjoy a good book, refreshing drink, or engaging conversation.

COZY UP WITH
Candles

Nothing makes a room more inviting than the soft flicker of candlelight. And, with so many different scents, colors, and containers to choose from, it's no wonder that candles are now a staple home accessory. Here I will share inspiration for how you can create a cozy glow that is perfect for a romantic dinner or relaxing night at home.

1. **Meet your match:** A lighter will get the job done, but the ritual of striking a match to light a candle evokes the senses and elevates the experience. Arrange your matches in a beautiful cloche or match holder (with a built-in striker).

2. **Set the scene:** Throw pillows are not just for the living room. If you want to create a truly intimate setting, bring soft cushions into your dining area. Then, dim the lights, open a bottle of wine, and light a candle—instant romance!

3. **Keep it simple:** Taper candles certainly have their place in the dining room, but I prefer votives when hosting a small dinner. Use a variety of container sizes and arrange them around your centerpiece for a look that is casual yet elegant.

Recipe for Romance

A dinner date does not have to be a formal affair.
Pick up some fresh flowers, arrange them in a
beautiful vase, light a few candles, and prepare
a simple meal. It's the company and ambiance
that make an evening memorable.

CREATE AN
Inspiring Workplace

People worldwide are working from home these days, and it is changing how we approach home design. As we convert spare bedrooms and finished basements, we must keep a few key points in mind. First, the home workspace should meet physical needs as well as practical needs. Second, the workspace should be well organized and well appointed.

1. Set yourself up for success: A home office needs to run as efficiently as a traditional workspace. Depending on the nature of your business, a small conference table and whiteboard may be suitable investments. Outfit the space with what you need, and your days will be more productive.

2. Get comfortable: Good seating is a must in any office. Look for desk chairs that allow your feet to rest flat on the floor while keeping your knees at hip level. If space allows, incorporate a variety of seating options, so there is an opportunity to move throughout the day.

3. Be inspired: One of the benefits of a home office is that you can express yourself more freely than you may be able to in a corporate setting. Surround yourself with inspiring books, plants, and other personal mementos. You'll be amazed at how much your environment affects your output and your happiness.

4. Tailor, tailor, tailor: A workspace must, of course, be functional, so be sure to think about what your particular job requires and tailor the space to your needs. In this sophisticated builder's office, the homeowner needed accessible storage for blueprints. We installed a beautiful racking system that keeps the plans within reach while making a handsome design statement.

A Workspace for Wellness

If you're busy enough to devote an entire room to a workspace, you will likely spend a lot of time working there. So, it's important to incorporate proper seating, lighting, and storage. Look for ergonomic chairs, install a combination of indirect and task lighting, and utilize closed storage, so you are not distracted by clutter.

MAKE A
Bed
(the Right Way)

Let's be honest. If you're old enough to be reading this book, chances are you've made your bed about a thousand times. But, we can all get stuck in a routine, so it's good to revisit the basics. A clean and well-made bed is essential to our physical and mental health.

1. Strip it down: How often do you wash your bedding? Experts recommend laundering pillowcases and sheets once a week, and comforters, mattress pads, and pillows every six months. Maintain this schedule for a healthful sleep environment.

2. Layer with love: A good-quality mattress is an investment, so start with a mattress pad to protect it. Next, place the fitted sheet on the bed, covering the corners fully. Spread the flat sheet on top (pattern side down) so the top edge is level with the top of the mattress. Tuck in the bottom of the sheet at the foot of the bed and secure the sides with hospital corners. Cover your pillows with cases. Now lay your comforter or bedspread over the sheets, positioning it so the edges are even on all sides. Finally, fold the flat sheet and comforter over at the top and place your sleeping pillows on the bed.

3. Add a pillow pop: Add personality and style to your bed with decorative throw pillows. I like to stand two large bolster pillows against the sleeping pillows, so they are upright and suitable for reading. Then, add two small rectangular pillows. If you have a neutral bedroom like the one shown here, look for pillows with patterns, pom-poms, and texture to add a pop to the room. Finish with a coordinating lumbar pillow.

4. Add warmth: Throw blankets are always a good idea! They add an extra layer of warmth in cool seasons and provide an additional opportunity to bring color, texture, and pattern into your space.

Sweet Dreams

Your bedroom environment has a significant impact on the quality of your sleep. To make the most of your resting hours, keep your bedroom clean and clutter-free. Avoid electronics before bed and keep the temperature cool. A neutral palette such as the one shown here evokes a peaceful feeling conducive to a good night's rest.

PLANT A
Terrarium

Terrariums are beautiful glass gardens that are easy to make and easy to maintain. They add charm to your home and make lovely gifts. The best part about making terrariums is that there are so many different ways to do it. Have fun picking out different shapes of glass containers and filling them with various combinations of plants.

1. **Gather your materials:** For this simple terrarium, I am using a base of potting soil, mood moss (green and white), a flowering succulent (kalanchoe), and crimson clover, which adds a dramatic color pop that coordinates with my interior décor.

2. **Add soil and plants:** Fill the bottom of your container with approximately 2 inches of moist potting soil. Pat it down and make small holes where you would like to place your plants. Remove the plants from their containers and loosen the roots if needed. Insert the plants into the holes, being sure to cover the roots with soil.

TIP: *Add a layer of gravel before the soil if your container does not have drainage.*

3. **Add color and green moss:** With your soil and base succulent in place, it's time to have fun. Here is where you can add color to your glass garden. I have added crimson clover, which gives the garden a bold pop of color and texture. Next, add the green moss around the plants.

4. **Add white moss and finish:** To complete your terrarium, insert small bunches of the white moss where you would like to add some contrast. If desired, add decorative stones or other accents to personalize your tiny garden. Place your terrarium in an area with filtered light, and water it as needed with a mister, atomizer, or spray bottle.

Let Nature Inspire You

The colors, shapes, and textures found in nature are an excellent source of inspiration for home décor. Take a camera or sketchbook on your next walk to record ideas.

PLANT A
Window
Box

Just outside my shop in Pennsylvania sits an adorable she-shed that my husband, Jeff, built for me when we started dating. The vintage windows, purchased at a local antique yard, are given new life with cheerful window boxes. It's incredible how seamlessly old and new can come together with a bit of creativity.

1. **Preparation is everything:** Your planting success is determined by how well you prepare your box. Make sure it is securely attached to its structure and has proper drainage. If there are no drainage holes, you can drill them into the bottom of the box or add a layer of gravel to avoid waterlogging.

2. **Start planting:** Fill your box with a good-quality potting mix and add your plants. Be sure to leave about 2 inches between each planting, and cover the root balls completely. Add a little more dirt if necessary and pat the potting mix down gently.

3. **Fill, thrill, spill:** Create visual interest in your window box, using the thrill, fill, spill technique. A thriller will add height and drama to your planting, a filler will add color and texture to your box, and a spiller will fall over the edge of your window box and give it balance.

4. **Handle with care:** Regular maintenance is critical for the health of your window box plantings, and it will also help promote big blooms. Check your window boxes daily and water them when the soil is dried out. Pinch spent blooms to encourage new growth.

Perfectly Imperfect

Some things just get better with age, and
that's certainly the case with the vintage Dutch
door that we repurposed for our garden shed.
Don't be afraid to mix old and new elements.
It's the best way to introduce character
and charm to any space!

SET THE MOOD WITH A
Creative Tablescape

Staying in is the new going out, and a dinner party is my favorite way to entertain guests in the home. A buffet is great for large crowds, but in my opinion, nothing beats the intimacy of gathering around the table with friends and family for a nourishing meal made with love. A creative tablescape with seasonal accents will set the tone for the evening.

1. **Place your centerpiece:** Flowers first, my friends! A beautiful bouquet set in the center of your table serves as the anchor for your tablescape. All other elements will work around it.

2. **Layer the dishware:** Even the most-casual dinners benefit from a table that is set in layers. Start with the dinner plate and folded napkin. Then, add a bread plate and salad bowl on top. The layers will give your table height and dimension.

3. **Add cutlery and glassware:** Place a salad fork and dinner fork on the left-hand side of the plate, and knife, spoon, and soup spoon to the right. Complete the setting by adding a water glass and wine glass (if wine is being served).

4. **Add the food!** Small snacks, fruit, and even bread can be laid on your table before the meal is served. Remember to add candles and light them just before your guests are seated. Bon appetit.

TIP: *Don't forget the music! Set the tone of your party with a curated playlist. Try old standards and Frank Sinatra during cocktail time and then switch over to classic jazz or mellow indie music when dinner is served.*

Make a Design Moment: Styling School with Sarah

Relaxed Dinner Party

Whether you are celebrating an important event or just gathering with friends and family, the dinner party is a wonderful way to welcome others to your home. The key to a memorable evening is making everyone feel comfortable. To set a casual tone at the table that still feels special, I like to mix natural textures and earthy ceramics with higher-end items in brass and gold.

STYLE A
Bar Cart

Oh, the versatile bar cart! There's a reason that everyone loves them. Bar carts are miniature vignettes where our collections can constantly be changing. Here, we will share ideas about how to style one for a swanky cocktail party, but you can use the basic building blocks to create an endless variety of themes.

1. **Pick and position your cart:** There are so many styles of bar carts on the market. Choose one that coordinates with your style, and position it against a statement art piece for maximum impact.

2. **Go for drama:** Start your styling by adding a large focal point on the top tier. I like to use fresh greenery and flowers. The height of the foliage will connect the cart to the wall art behind it, making a seamless design transition.

3. **Add key pieces:** The first elements to arrange are your essential items. Here we have placed our wine on the top shelf and glasses on the bottom. In between, we layered in books to balance the look and add interest. A chunky mortar and pestle adds a culinary flair and is handy when preparing craft cocktails.

4. **Accessorize:** Expand upon your theme with coordinating accessories. I added a handsome jar of olives, a polished-brass ice bucket, beverage mixers, and fresh fruit for our cocktail party theme. Have fun personalizing your cart and enjoy the party. Cheers!

Raise the Bar

When was the last time you upgraded your bar accessories? If you're like most people, it's been awhile! So take inventory before your next party and replace anything necessary. It's incredible how one glamourous piece can elevate the entire vignette (like the polished-brass ice bucket on this cart).

STYLE A
Coffee Table

Don't underestimate the impact of a well-outfitted coffee table. This hardworking piece of furniture is a focal point of your main living space. It multifunctions as a gathering spot for conversation, a place to rest food and beverages, and a relaxation hub where favorite books, television remotes, and handy coasters are stored.

1. Look for layers: When purchasing a coffee table, I recommend a tiered design. Large baskets placed on lower shelves are great for storing television remotes, kid's toys, and other necessary but not-so-pretty items.

2. Add a vase: Houseplants and fresh flowers arranged in beautiful ceramic pots add life, character, and charm to any room. It's always my starting point.

3. Bring on the books: Books capture our imagination and allow us to indulge in our interests. Arrange a few cherished volumes on your coffee table, so they are always within reach.

4. Add the accents: Here's where you can have fun. Add objects of art or a small bowl filled with wooden beads, seashells, polished stones, or other items that are meaningful to you and your family.

Relaxed Refinement

Modern homemaking is all about creating
a home environment that's beautiful enough to
welcome guests but comfortable enough for the
inhabitants to truly relax. Plush furnishing and
natural materials are timeless elements that
will help you accomplish both goals.

STYLE A COZY
Guest Room

Surprise—company is coming! Is your guest room guest-ready? Here are a few tips to cozy up a spare bedroom to make sure your guests feel welcome. A clean and serene palette always provides comfort, especially when paired with soft blankets, ample pillows, and a thoughtful gift basket.

1. **Layer on the pillows:** Weary travelers will be happy to rest their heads on a bed that is layered with soft pillows. Use good sleeping pillows as the foundation and add throw pillows in various sizes for extra comfort.

2. **Provision the nightstand:** Your guests will be grateful that they don't have to find their way to the kitchen in the middle of the night, when you provide them with bottled water. Add a glass decanter and fresh florals for an elegant touch.

3. **Provide storage:** Clean out a few drawers or the entire dresser so that guests can unpack upon arrival. Then, stow suitcases and overnight bags in the closet.

4. **When in doubt, add blankets:** Everyone has different temperature preferences, so make sure you have extra blankets available for chilly nights (or hot summer ones when the air conditioner is on).

TIP: The key to hospitality is anticipating your guests, needs and providing them in advance. Frame your Wi-Fi password, provide interesting reading materials, and stock the bathroom with travel-sized essentials in case they forgot toiletries.

The Art of the Gift Basket

When overnight guests come to visit, make them feel special with a curated gift basket filled. I love to fill mine with tea, fresh fruit, a sweet or salty snack, and scented candle. Get creative and let your guests, interests inspire you.

STYLE A
Mantel

A fireplace is a major focal point in any room. So, if you are lucky enough to have one, it's worth investing time in styling its mantel beautifully. First, consider your fireplace's architectural details, and then select décor pieces that complement them. For this historical fireplace, I wanted to let the gorgeous hexagonal brickwork shine, so I intentionally kept the design scaled back.

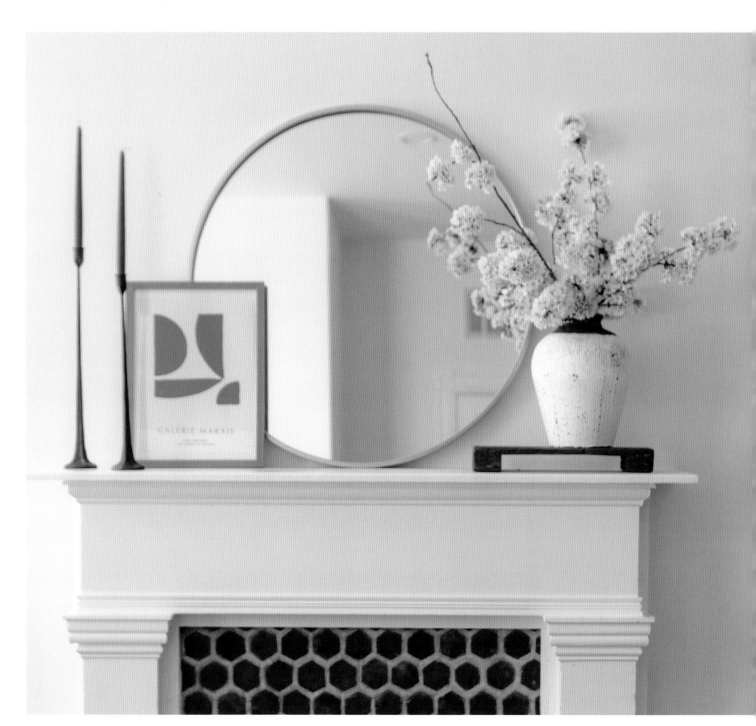

1. **Make a plan:** Remove all existing items from your mantel. Step about 6 feet back and assess your situation. Is your fireplace centered on the wall? Are there built-in sconces that you need to incorporate into the design? Think about colors, shapes, and sizes.

2. **Position the anchor:** The anchor is your focal point. It's the piece that all other elements support. Here I have chosen a round mirror that complements the brick pattern on the fireplace surround.

3. **Add seasonal elements:** The mantel is a beautiful place to showcase seasonal decor. I love to fill a textured vase with the leaves, stems, and flower that are in bloom at any given time of the year. It's a creative and inexpensive way to freshen up your room.

4. **Balance it out:** It's typically best to work in odd numbers when designing. And, here, you can see I have balanced out the mirror, flower vase, and pedestal with candlesticks and a framed art print. Notice how the pieces work together to fill the space without distracting from the overall beauty of the fireplace.

When Less is More

Sometimes it's best to leave your mantle undecorated, as we did in this living room, where we did not want to draw attention away from the show-stopping stone wall.

STYLE A
Bookcase

Whether you are looking for a classic case to organize a library or a closed-door cabinet to show off and protect a favorite collection, a bookcase is an essential piece of furniture for any home. In this project, I'll show you some basic layering techniques to fill your case with style and sophistication, all while being functional.

1. **State your case:** There are a seemingly endless variety of bookcases on the market. So, research before buying. Think about how you will use the case, and measure your space to determine a suitable size. If you're using your case to organize often-used items, open shelving is a good idea. If you want to show off a beloved collection, go for closed glass doors, as shown in this picture.

2. **Build a foundation:** Place one large piece on each shelf to create a strong foundation. Notice how the vintage stone sculpture ties in with the adjacent planter, and the wooden box ties in with the wicker basket. The textured vase on top brings the gray-brown palette together.

3. **Build with books:** Curate a collection of your favorite books and arrange them in neat stacks on each shelf of your cabinet. Lay them flat to protect their spines and add height to your display.

4. **Bring in color:** A neutral palette comes to life with texture and greenery. Incorporate a potted plant into your design. Don't worry if you don't have a green thumb. Use faux plants or dried flowers, like the ones shown here!

Make a Statement

All it takes is one amazing piece of furniture to transform an entire space like the black bookcase in this small living room. Find a statement piece that you love, and design your other elements around it.

WARM UP A
White Room

Come to the white side! Do you love the look of a white room but feel terrified that it will look cold and sterile in your home? Have no fear. A white space can be warm, welcoming, and even family-friendly when you plan properly. I'll show you how to go from white to warm with soft furnishings, luxe drapery, and woven textures in this project. Color trends come and go, but white is forever!

1. Soft place to land: Soft and plush furnishings like this cozy armchair are essential in a white room. They invite relaxation and make the space feel cozy. Look for options with deep seats that allow your friends and family to sink into them for long conversations.

2. Something living: Houseplants and flowers are magic. They make any space come alive and are especially effective in white rooms. Use textured pots or vases to add additional warmth to the room.

3. Go natural: The warm tones of wood and wicker instantly warm up a white space. Look for furniture with wood accents and decorate the room with woven baskets, wood beads, and other natural elements.

4. Be bold: Black adds contrast and sophistication to any room, especially a white one. Notice how the black door and black hardware on the wicker basket work together to balance the otherwise neutral space.

Transform
with Texture

Texture brings a room to life and keeps it from feeling flat. You can introduce texture into your space by layering fabrics and accessorizing with natural materials like rattan, stone, and wood.

MAKE A
Market Bouquet

Flowers are always a good idea! Whether you are looking for a hostess gift, holiday gift, or a pretty pick-me-up, fresh flowers fit the bill. I love to combine a few bouquets from the local farmstand and rewrap them to elevate the look. If you are harvesting flowers from your garden, remember to clip each of the three f's: flowers, filler, and foliage!

1. **Prep and arrange the flowers:** Unwrap, organize, and trim each stem to fit onto the kraft paper. Remove leaves from the lower half of each stem and assemble your bouquet. Secure the bundle with floral tape.

2. **Position the flowers:** Lay the bouquet diagonally on the kraft paper as shown.

3. **Prep the paper:** Pull the bottom of the kraft paper up to the base of the flower heads and hold it in place with your thumb.

4. **Wrap the bouquet:** Pull the left side of the paper over the bouquet, covering it completely. Then, pull the right side of the paper around to wrap the front. If desired, you can secure the bundle with a staple in the upper left corner.

5. **Tie with twine:** Here is the fun part. Wrap your bouquet with twine and tie it into a bow. If desired, you can also use a coordinating ribbon. Have fun and get creative. Trim any excess twine, and voilà, your market bouquet is complete!

TIP: *If you expect that your bouquet will remain out of water for longer than one hour, you can wrap the stems with a damp paper towel and insert them into a small plastic baggie to keep them hydrated.*

Boost Your Mood
with Flowers

Did you know that flowers have been proven to decrease stress and increase happiness? It's true! So, that's a good reason to keep fresh-cut blooms in your home year-round.

Wrap a Gift

It's nice to have a beautifully wrapped present to welcome guests when they visit. It shows you anticipated their arrival and are happy to see them. Here we will review the proper techniques for wrapping presents so you can avoid the last-minute dash of throwing something in a gift bag! After all, love is in the details.

1. Gather materials: Gather your gift, a box, wrapping paper, scissors, tape, and ribbon or twine. Tissue paper or other filler is also helpful to have on hand.

2. Box it: If there is a price tag, remove it and place your gift inside the box.

3. Let's roll: Roll the wrapping paper out (pattern side down) on a flat surface. Place your box topside down and center it.

4. Trim to size: Using sharp scissors, cut a piece of paper about twice as long as your box.

5. Meet in the middle: Fold two ends of the paper up and over the sides of the box to meet in the middle. The paper should overlap by a few inches (trim if needed).

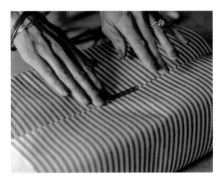

6. Tape it up: Secure the overlapping paper with tape. I am using translucent black washi tape to add a pop of modernity to this otherwise classic paper.

7. Fold and crease: Fold the top of the wrapping paper down and press it against the box, creasing the corners.

8. Press and crease again: Fold the corners in and crease them along the bottom edge. Lift the bottom of the wrapping paper and press it against the side of the box, covering the corners. Secure with tape. Repeat steps 7 and 8 on the other side of the box.

9. Get creative: Finish the package with a bow or ribbon. I like to use twine and tuck a dried flower on top for an unexpected and unique presentation.

The Hostess Gift

When you attend a dinner party or other engagement in someone's home, it's nice to bring a hostess gift. Small items like food, flowers, and wine all are excellent choices.

Make a Plan:
Creative Tools for Organizing

A clean home is a serene home! In this section, you'll get handy information to help you organize household chores and events so that life can run more effortlessly. This is your opportunity to make a plan and get organized!

Keeping Things Tidy

A clean home is a calm home. Keep yours nice and tidy by following the daily, weekly, and monthly checklists provided below. Then, be sure to embark on seasonal deep cleaning to keep your home (and the people in it) happy and healthy.

Daily Cleaning Checklist

- ☐ Clean coffee maker
- ☐ Disinfect sinks, counters, and often-used handles
- ☐ Make beds
- ☐ Open and file mail
- ☐ Put away children's toys
- ☐ Remove trash and recycling as needed
- ☐ Sweep kitchen floor
- ☐ Tidy common areas
- ☐ Wash and put away dishes
- ☐ Wash, fold, and put away laundry

Weekly Cleaning Checklist

- ☐ Clean kitchen appliances
- ☐ Clean out refrigerator
- ☐ Dust surfaces and ceiling fans
- ☐ Polish mirrors
- ☐ Scrub tubs, toilets, and bathroom sinks
- ☐ Vacuum rugs and mop floors
- ☐ Wash sheets and change bedding
- ☐ Wash, fold, and put away towels and other house linens

Monthly

- ☐ Clean and disinfect kitchen cabinet doors
- ☐ Clean staircases and spindles
- ☐ Scrub bathroom tiles and grout
- ☐ Vacuum soft furnishings (including under cushions)
- ☐ Wipe down baseboards

Deep Cleaning

- ☐ Clean dryer vents
- ☐ Clean oven interior
- ☐ Clean under and behind kitchen appliances
- ☐ Clean window blinds
- ☐ Declutter and donate unused items
- ☐ Defrost and clean freezer
- ☐ Dust lampshades
- ☐ Vacuum mattresses
- ☐ Wash or dry-clean window coverings
- ☐ Wash pillows
- ☐ Wash shower curtains and liners
- ☐ Wash windows
- ☐ Wipe down walls

Essential Tools

- ☐ Broom and dustpan
- ☐ Bucket
- ☐ Extendable duster
- ☐ Microfiber cloths
- ☐ Mop
- ☐ Sponge
- ☐ Spray bottles
- ☐ Squeegee
- ☐ Vacuum
- ☐ White cleaning rags

Declutter Checklist

Clutter can creep up on you quickly. To avoid the feeling of overwhelmingness that comes with disorganization, try these tips to keep your main living spaces neat, tidy, and pared down.

Bathroom

- ☐ Designate a vanity drawer for hair styling tools and accessories
- ☐ Fold towels neatly; keep extras in the linen closet
- ☐ Remove expired products from the medicine cabinet
- ☐ Stow personal care items in drawers or baskets

Bedroom

- ☐ Donate books that you no longer want to read
- ☐ Go through dresser drawers and discard unused or unwanted clothing
- ☐ Go through nightstand drawers and discard anything no longer needed
- ☐ Make the bed
- ☐ Put laundry away immediately after washing and drying
- ☐ Stow extra blankets and pillows in the linen closet

Closet

- ☐ Donate, recycle, or sell unused garments
- ☐ Install organizers for accessories like scarves and handbags
- ☐ Organize garments into sections (blouses, pants, sweaters, etc.)
- ☐ Organize shoes by color and season
- ☐ Stow rarely used items on the top shelf
- ☐ Tidy nightstand and dresser surfaces

Kitchen

- ☐ Consolidate cleaning products
- ☐ Designate a spot for mail, and file or shred it regularly
- ☐ Establish a charging station for cell phones and other electronics
- ☐ Hang hooks to organize keys
- ☐ Organize drawers by category (plastic bags, spices, utensils, utility, etc.)
- ☐ Organize fruit and snacks in baskets
- ☐ Reduce refrigerator magnets
- ☐ Remove expired food items from the pantry and refrigerator
- ☐ Stow rarely used small appliances

Living Room

- ☐ Hang coats and bags in the closet
- ☐ Keep television remote controls in a basket
- ☐ Put children's toys in baskets when not in use
- ☐ Remove any outdated electronics, cables, or cords
- ☐ Remove broken, unused, or no-longer-loved items
- ☐ Return out-of-place items to their proper room
- ☐ Straighten the coffee table regularly

Mudroom or Entryway

- ☐ Fix or discard any broken items (such as umbrellas or sporting equipment)
- ☐ Go through all drawers and discard any unwanted or unused items
- ☐ Remove out-of-season coats, shoes, and bags for long-term storage
- ☐ Return out-of-place items to their proper spaces

Pantry Checklist

Avoid the weekly mad dash to the grocery store with a well-stocked pantry. Of course, everyone's needs are different, so use this list as a starting point to ensure that you have essential items on hand.

Baking Supplies and Sweeteners

- [ ] Baking powder
- [ ] Baking soda
- [ ] Cocoa powder
- [ ] Condensed milk
- [ ] Confectioners' sugar
- [ ] Cornmeal
- [ ] Cornstarch
- [ ] Dark brown sugar
- [ ] Flour (all-purpose)
- [ ] Granulated sugar
- [ ] Honey
- [ ] Light brown sugar
- [ ] Maple syrup
- [ ] Vanilla extract

Oils and Vinegars

- [ ] Apple cider vinegar
- [ ] Balsamic vinegar
- [ ] Canola oil
- [ ] Extra virgin olive oil
- [ ] Red wine vinegar
- [ ] Vegetable oil
- [ ] White vinegar

Herbs, Seasonings, and Spices

- [ ] Basil
- [ ] Bay leaves
- [ ] Black pepper
- [ ] Bouillon
- [ ] Cayenne (ground)
- [ ] Chili powder
- [ ] Cinnamon
- [ ] Cumin
- [ ] Curry powder
- [ ] Dill
- [ ] Garlic powder
- [ ] Ginger
- [ ] Kosher salt
- [ ] Nutmeg
- [ ] Oregano
- [ ] Paprika
- [ ] Red pepper flakes
- [ ] Rosemary
- [ ] Sage
- [ ] Salt
- [ ] Sesame seeds
- [ ] Thyme

Grains and Starches

- [ ] Beans
- [ ] Breadcrumbs
- [ ] Brown rice
- [ ] Couscous
- [ ] Crackers
- [ ] Long-grain rice
- [ ] Panko
- [ ] Pasta (various)
- [ ] Quinoa
- [ ] White rice

Nuts, Snacks, and Staples

- [ ] Almonds
- [ ] Almond butter
- [ ] Bread
- [ ] Cereal
- [ ] Cookies
- [ ] Fruit jams
- [ ] Oatmeal
- [ ] Peanuts
- [ ] Peanut butter
- [ ] Popcorn
- [ ] Pretzels
- [ ] Rolled oats
- [ ] Tortilla
- [ ] Walnuts

Canned Goods (and Jars)

- [ ] Beans
- [ ] Beef stock
- [ ] Chicken stock
- [ ] Diced tomatoes
- [ ] Pickles
- [ ] Olives
- [ ] Tomato paste
- [ ] Tomato sauce
- [ ] Tuna
- [ ] Vegetable stock

Condiments, Dressings, and Sauces

- [ ] Barbecue sauce
- [ ] Hot sauce
- [ ] Ketchup
- [ ] Mayonnaise
- [ ] Mustard
- [ ] Salad dressings
- [ ] Salsa
- [ ] Soy sauce
- [ ] Worcestershire sauce
- [ ] Vinaigrette

Glassware

Drinking vessels come in a variety of shapes and sizes. Each one is specifically designed to complement a particular beverage's characteristics. For example, martini glasses have sloped sides to hold cocktail garnishes on long skewers. Use this handy reference to ensure that you're serving cocktails, mocktails, wine, and spirits in the right glass!

Highball	Collins	Weizenbier	Pilsner	Pint	Mug
Irish Coffee	Old-Fashioned	Rocks	Tumbler	Cosmopolitan	Martini
Margarita	Hurricane	Sour	Milkshake	Red wine	White wine
Rose wine	Port wine	Sherry	Flute	Coupe	Goblet
Chalice	Snifter	Tulip	Cordial	Liqueur	Shot

Table Setting

Some things never go out of style, and that's certainly the case with a beautifully set table. Although you may not need to break the china out regularly, it is fun to host a formal event every once in a while. And, when you do, this chart will show you precisely where to put all of those knives, forks, and spoons. Love is in the details, friends!

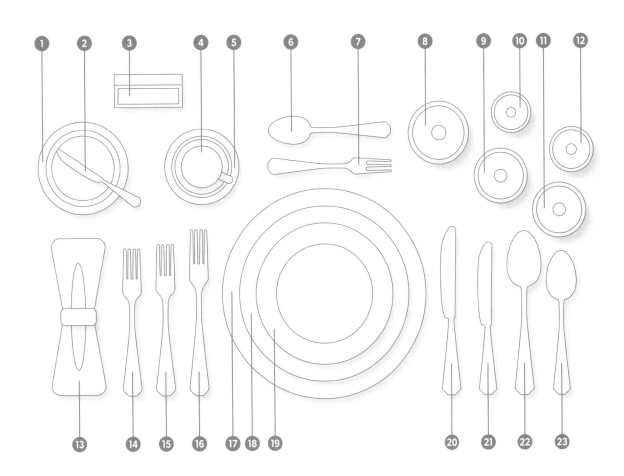

1. Bread plate
2. Butter knife
3. Place card
4. Coffee cup
5. Coffee saucer
6. Dessert spoon

7. Dessert fork
8. Water goblet
9. Red wine glass
10. Champagne flute
11. White wine glass
12. Sherry glass

13. Napkin
14. Salad fork
15. Fish fork
16. Dinner fork
17. Dinner plate
18. Soup bowl

19. Salad plate
20. Dinner knife
21. Salad knife
22. Dinner spoon
23. Soup spoon

Party Checklist

The key to a successful event is planning. Review this checklist before your next soiree to make sure you that you can spend more time with friends and family and less time stressing out in the kitchen!

Key Tasks

- [ ] Establish a budget
- [ ] Set date, place, and time
- [ ] Plan the guest list
- [ ] Consider and plan for parking
- [ ] Send invitations (with RSVP date)
- [ ] Set the menu and associated shopping lists
- [ ] Place orders, secure provisions
- [ ] Plan table and food layout
- [ ] Organize entertainment or create a playlist
- [ ] Plan a toast or speech if appropriate
- [ ] Organize, order, or make favors if desired
- [ ] Hire a photographer if desired
- [ ] Tally RSVPs and follow up with guests as needed
- [ ] Clean and organize your house (plan ahead for coat storage, gift table, etc.)

Plan the Party Schedule

- [ ] Guests arrive
- [ ] Appetizers and drinks
- [ ] Toast
- [ ] Meal
- [ ] Gifts
- [ ] Dessert
- [ ] Send-off

Essential Items

- [ ] Aluminum foil
- [ ] Cake stands
- [ ] Chafing dishes (if desired) and fuel
- [ ] Dish detergent
- [ ] Drink dispensers
- [ ] Ice (and coolers if needed)
- [ ] Napkins (dinner and dessert)
- [ ] Paper towels
- [ ] Party décor
- [ ] Plastic storage bags
- [ ] Plates, cups, cutlery
- [ ] Dessert plates and coffee cups
- [ ] Serving platters and bowls
- [ ] Serving utensils
- [ ] To-go containers
- [ ] Toilet paper
- [ ] Trash bags

Party Ideas

- [ ] Farm-to-Table Dinner Party
- [ ] Friend or Family Reunion Party
- [ ] Low Country Seafood Boil Party
- [ ] Neighborhood Block Party
- [ ] Paint (or Craft) Party
- [ ] Small-Plate Appetizer Party
- [ ] Summer Garden Party
- [ ] Wine and Cheese Pairing Party

Furniture Styles

Picking out furniture can be overwhelming! Use this handy reference to guide you. First, look at the designs to find out what style best suits your décor direction, then search catalogs and other resources by name to find the perfect piece for your home.

Sofa Design Styles

Lawson

English Rolled Arm

Tuxedo

Mid-century Modern

Sectional

Chesterfield

Accent Chair Styles

Club

Slipper

Wing

Mid-century Modern

Barrel

Notes

Index

A

accent chairs, *24*

accessorize, *21, 51, 139*

al fresco dining, *109*

antique mismatched chairs, *79*

art, *7, 11, 13, 36, 48, 51, 54, 57, 95, 139, 143, 148, 151*

B

bar cart, *30, 138–139*

bathroom, *11, 13, 15, 17–18, 21, 147, 173, 175*

bedroom, *15, 23–24, 27, 35–36, 118, 123–124, 146, 175*

bedside table, *24*

blankets, *23, 39, 123, 146–147, 175*

bookcase, *48, 154–156*

bunk beds, *39*

C

candles, *7, 13, 17, 21, 114–115, 117, 135*

ceramics, *10, 136*

ceremony marker, *73*

child's room, *35, 39*

children's birthday party, *97*

clean home, *171, 173*

cleaning checklist, *173*

closed storage, *57, 120*

coffee table, *7, 11, 13, 51, 142–143, 175*

counter, *21, 42, 63, 173*

D

declutter checklist, *175*

dessert bar, *99*

dining room design, *29*

dinner party, *107, 134, 136, 169, 183*

dishware, *29, 135*

F

floor space, *39, 66*

floral centerpiece, *106, 109*

flower-arranging party, *81, 87*

flower bar, *87*

fresh flowers, *7, 10–11, 29, 81, 106, 117, 143, 162*

furniture styles, *185*

G

garages, *111*

gift basket, *146, 148*

glass shower enclosure, *21*

glass-front cabinets, *42*

glassware, *135, 179*

guest room, *146*

H

hangers, *35*

high-arc faucet, *41*

holiday season, *89, 95*

hooks, *35, 54, 57, 63, 175*

hostess gift, *162, 169*

I

inspiring workplace, *118*

L

laundry, *35, 66, 69, 173, 175*

living rooms, *47*

locker room, *57*

M

make a bed, *122*

mantel, *150–151*

market bouquet, *162–163*

mirrors, *11, 48, 173*

mudroom, *53–54, 57, 175*

O

organizing, *54, 65, 173, 175, 177, 179, 181, 183, 185*

outdoor living, *113*

P

pantry checklist, *177*

party checklist, *183*

pillow, *10–11, 23–24, 36, 47, 115, 123, 146–147, 173, 175*

plants, *10, 27, 57–60, 63, 119, 126–127, 131, 155*

potting shed, *59–60, 63*

R

rug, *27, 39, 51, 173*

S

sculptural chairs, *48*

statement piece, *27, 156*

T

table décor, *29, 73*

table setting, *181*

tablescape, *134–135*

terrarium, *126–127*

throw blankets, *23, 123*

throw pillows, *47, 115, 123, 147*

U

utility room, *65–66, 69*

W

wall-mounted dryer rack, *66*

wallpaper, *11, 69*

white room, *158–159*

window box, *60, 130–131*

SARAH ROSE INCH is the creative force behind Gray Apple Design, a rapidly growing interior design firm. Additionally, she is the proprietor of Gray Apple Market, a curated boutique of beautiful home goods. Together, she and her husband own and operate Inch & Co., a design and build firm recently recognized on the *Inc. 5000 Fastest-Growing Companies in America* list and Hueter's Greenhouses. Sarah recently completed shooting a test pilot for HGTV. Learn more at @grayappledesign, @grayapplemarket.

*For my father, the consummate craftsman
who inspired my love of design and
taught me the difference between building a house
and making a home. Without you,
this book would not be possible.*

BETTER DAY BOOKS®
HAPPY · CREATIVE · CURATED®

Business is personal at Better Day Books. We were founded on the belief that all people are creative and that making things by hand is inherently good for us. It's important to us that you know how much we appreciate your support. The book you are holding in your hands was crafted with the artistic passion of the author and brought to life by a team of wildly enthusiastic creatives who believed it could inspire you. If it did, please drop us a line and let us know about it. Connect with us on Instagram, post a photo of your art, and let us know what other creative pursuits you are interested in learning about. It all matters to us. You're kind of a big deal.

it's a good day to have a better day!®

www.betterdaybooks.com

better_day_books